Footprints on
My Heart

Footprints on My Heart

by

Patricia Kirwin Henderson

RoseDog Books

PITTSBURGH, PENNSYLVANIA 15222

ISBN: 978-1-4349-9549-0
Printed in the United States of America

First Printing

For more information or to order additional books, please contact:
RoseDog Books
701 Smithfield Street
Pittsburgh, Pennsylvania 15222
U.S.A.
1-800-834-1803
www.rosedogbookstore.com

This book is dedicated to my loving husband Bill, who encouraged me to take on this project. Also, my beautiful children, my son Billy married to Maria, my daughter Kelly married to Adam, my son Joe married to Jacque, and my son Scott...also, my grandchildren, Billy, Kayla, Brian, Jason and Sophia.
They are my heart.
All of them have been through this with me and have been very supportive. I love each and every one of them with all my heart.

I wrote this book so that I could share my story about my loved ones and all the ways they have used to let me know they are around me in Spirit. For all those that have lost a loved one, I hope this book serves to bring some comfort knowing that their loved ones are always around them too, guiding them all the time. They are just a thought away. I have experienced this first hand. I am not very religious, but I am very Spiritual and feel truly blessed to have experienced this journey.

They have truly left their footprints on my heart.

Although they left this world
Although they did indeed, depart
They never really left
For they left footprints on my heart.
When I hear a certain song
Or see a butterfly on high
I know my loved ones are not really gone
They are still coming by.
When in my dreams I see my mom and dad
I know they truly comfort me and I am truly glad.
Our loved ones do not really leave
They visit as often as they can
So please do not grieve for you will see them *again*.
Although they left this world
Although they did indeed depart
My loved ones did not really leave
For they left footprints on my heart.

Written by Lana Director my good friend.
She encouraged me to get this book published.
Thank you Lana!

No longer in my life:

My father Joseph...passed November 23, 1969.
My mother Winifred...passed January 3, 1985.
My siblings:
Margaret (Margie)... passed March 1, 1994.
William (Willie)...passed February 5, 1996.
Joseph (Joe)... passed March 15, 1999
James (Jimmy)...passed February 24, 2000
Maureen...passed Oct 24, 2005

There are only two of us left now...me and my brother
Tommy.
I am 63 years old and Tommy is 64. He resides in upstate
New York and I live in New Jersey with my husband of
forty five years, Bill, a son, and our beautiful Cocka-Poo
Reilly.
I have two other sons and a daughter all married. I also
have
five grandchildren.
I love music and have enjoyed ten years in my drum corp,
The Sons And Daughters Of The Ex5[th] Regiment Fife and
Drum Corp. I play both Fife and Drum and really enjoyed
it
while it lasted. Presently, I love to listen to music, dance,
read
books, cook, go on my computer and spend time with
those I love.

I was born March 10, 1946, the sixth
child of Joseph and

Winifred Kirwin. I had a very happy
childhood and loved

all my other siblings. My parents were
not wealthy in the

monetary sense but we seven children
always had a nice

clean home, food on the table and
everything else we needed.

We were raised all for one and one for
all.

My father worked for the city of
Paterson where we lived and

drove a cab for extra income. He also
was a musician who played
trumpet in an Orchestra at a Night Club
on occasion. He also

had a love for Martial Music and that
led him to join a Drum Corp,

the Ex-Fifth Regiment Field Music where
he played Bugle and Bass

Drum. He passed this love of the music
onto my brothers. Two

of them joined this drum corp at a young
age and the family would

all go to the Parades starting on
Memorial Day which was then called

Decoration Day, right up until December.

My father was stern with us and taught
us to be honest and trustworthy

and to always watch out for each other.

My mother was a "gentle giant" ...she was
very soft spoken and a real Lady

but we knew when she meant business. My
mother was a Registered Nurse who

worked as long as I can remember. How
she did that with seven children

to raise is nothing short of miraculous.
She was a very kind and compassionate

mother. I remember having the Measles
and had to stay home from school. My

mother kept me in bed and made sure I
was comfortable and kept the room dark...

that's something you had to do in those
days, something about the light being

harmful to your eyes. She would come
into the room quietly to check on me and

would bring food in on a tray...she
always made sure our needs were met.

Every night in our house, supper was
like a Thanksgiving dinner. She always

made dessert too like bread pudding or a
cake or something. She kept an

immaculate home and expected nothing
less from her children. If my older

brother and sister were working when we
sat down to eat, she would make them

a plate and keep it warm until they came
home.

She always taught us to listen to our
older brothers and my older sister.

The oldest was my brother Joe, next was
my sister Maureen, then Willie

James, Tommy, me and Margie who was the
baby.

We all got along well and were very
close. God forbid if anybody gave us

younger ones a hard time, they'd have to
answer to the "clan" as we were

often called. We had a lot of relatives
too, my father had four sisters

and my mother had three sisters
and a brother, so we had lots of cousins

in the family. At that time we lived in
a housing project and the memories

I have of those times are some of the
best in my life. We are Irish so there

was always music and dancing...whether
it be the record player or my father

and the boys playing instruments. My
mother played piano...we all loved

music, singing and dancing. Music was
always a priority in our house.

Every Christmas, the relatives would all
come over that night and there would

be a party...everybody having a great
time...kids and all.

There were tons of kids to play with in
the project...it was like a big family.

All of my aunts and uncles owned their
own homes but none of them had seven

kids to feed and clothe, or the memories
that come when there is a large

family. They may have had more in a
monetary sense, but that's where it
stops.

We were much closer siblings than my
cousins were. I can remember not
wanting

to sleep anywhere but home. I had a
cousin who I was close to, she was an
only child, and always wanted me to sleep
over. After awhile I relented but I can

remember being so homesick that I
couldn't wait to go home. I would never
let

on how I felt because I didn't want to
hurt her feelings or my aunt's because

she was my favorite aunt. None of the
cousins slept over our house because we

didn't have the room. I always felt as
though they looked down on us a little

because we lived in a project, but they
all wanted to hang out with us...their

"project cousins" because we always had
fun. We always had something going

on whether it be a stick ball game, jump
rope, hide and go seek, music, you
name it.

This is why I miss my brothers and
sisters so much. I feel as though a
part

of me is missing and at this point in my
life, I am married and have four

beautiful children and five beautiful
grandchildren and this emptiness has nothing to
do with any of that. We were just close

and had a lot in common and they all
passed very young and sudden.

There is no such thing as closure,
you just get used to the pain and learn

to accept it as time goes by. I don't
remember exactly how I got into all

the little signs that our loved ones
leave. I only know that there really

is an after life and that we don't die,
we pass over into another Dimension

and our Spirit or Soul lives on and on
and it's that Spirit that can make these

signs all happen. I remember being
outside on my deck and this Butterfly would

come at me very close to my face. I
would shoo it away but it would keep

coming at me and I would just keep
shooing it away...then I found out that

that is one way our loved ones use to
come and say "Hi".

Now I welcome them and it's not unusual
for me to see groups of four flying

near me. I've also had instances where
had my lights and my Television

go on and off by themselves...sometimes
the channels changing as if someone

was holding the button down...it's all
ways they use to let you know they
are with us.

That's why I needed to write this book
about my loved ones...they left

their footprints on my heart, never to
be erased by death.

November 23, 1969 was a Saturday...a
really nice day. I was visiting my
friend

who lived up the street near my
parents' house. I always stopped in on
Saturday

to see my parents but I didn't make it
this day. I was having my sister
Maureen

and her husband over that night for a
few drinks and a few laughs. My visit
at

my friend's house ran longer than
expected and I had to get ready for
tonight,

so I went home and figured I'd stop up
my parents' house tomorrow.

We had a great time that night with my
sister and brother-in-law...we laughed

so much our sides ached. Whenever the
family was together and we'd get to

laughing hysterically my sister would
always say, "Something's gonna happen".

We just ignored it but this time
something did happen. As they left for
the

night, it was around midnight, we
noticed a ring around the moon and we
got

so silly laughing about that and again
my sister, "Something's gonna happen".

As I lay in bed trying to get to sleep,
I wondered why I couldn't sleep...I

kept thinking that maybe my newborn baby
daughter would get sick because

she did have Conjunctivitis and all this
was playing in my head. With that

the phone rang...although I was awake, I
froze and shook my husband who jumped

up and went in the kitchen to answer it.
I don't know why I froze, I was just

spooked although I don't know why.

I was sure it would be a wrong number,
at this hour who could it be? I heard

my husband saying, "Oh no.. Oh my
God...ok I'll be right up". I jumped up
now

my heart racing knowing something was
very wrong. I said, "What"? "What is

going on"? He said, "That was your
mother, it's your Dad, your Mother
thinks

he died, there's an Ambulance coming".
"Oh my God" I screamed. My husband

was going up there, it was only up the street.
I couldn't go because I had
a toddler and a newborn and it was the
wee hours of the morning. I told him

to please call me when he gets there and knows any-
thing.
I'm now pacing and

ran into my parlor where I watched out
the window as the Ambulance went flying

up the street praying they could save my
father. He had a few heart attacks

before so I knew this was serious. I
paced and cried and prayed but my father

passed away actually before the
Ambulance arrived. Talk about tomorrow

never comes. I was so mad at myself for
not stopping there yesterday. In

fact, all of my siblings planned on
stopping that afternoon but they all got

detoured too and figured they would stop
on Sunday.

We were all wracked with grief...he was
only fifty seven years old.

About a month after he died, I got up to
feed and change my newborn daughter

and discovered that a lamp in my parlor
was on. I just turned it off when I

finished and went back to bed. I am the
type that checks and double checks to

be sure the doors are locked, Television
off and lights are out, so this

baffled me. The next morning, I asked
my husband if he had gotten up during

the night to watch TV and left the lamp
on...he said, "No". For two more

nights when I got up with my newborn
daughter, that lamp was on. There

certainly had to be an explanation for this
and the only one I could think

of was it had to be my almost three year
old son. The next day I was holding

my daughter on the couch and my son was
watching television. I asked him to

please turn the lamp on. This lamp was
centered on top of the TV and was

quite tall, brass with a skeleton like
decorative key that was welded onto the

brass in the front of the lamp. The
three way on/off switch was in the back

opposite but even with the key. First
thing he did was to grab a chair from

the Dining Room which was just off the
parlor and dragged it to the front of

the TV and stood on it and tried to turn
the key! He kept saying, "I can't

turn it on". I knew that he could never
have pulled this off in the wee small

hours of the morning without the whole
house hearing all that noise and what

sense would it make anyway....but I had
to explore every possible explanation.

The first night I had found this lamp
on, I had gone up to my mother's

apartment earlier. She had called all
her children on the phone and said

she was breaking up the apartment and
would be moving in with my aunt and

uncle and wanted us to pick out some
pictures of my father that we could

have as a keepsake. I picked out two
that I especially liked and when I

came home, I hung them right up in the
parlor.

I later learned that our loved ones are
always around us in Spirit and can

communicate with us using electronics
etc. I felt very comforted learning
this

because I never got to say goodbye to my
father.

Also, my mother was staying with me and
my husband at our apartment which

was just down he street from where they
lived. She would be staying until

after the Funeral. My mother needed her
good black dress coat for the Wake

and Funeral. My husband went up the
street to their apartment, we actually

had lived in that apartment before my
parents moved in, so he was very

familiar with the place. He opened the
door, flipped on the wall switch that

the lamp was hooked up to and went to
the closet on the opposite side of the

parlor to get the coat. As he opened
the closet door, the parlor lamp went

for a second or two and then came back
on and stayed on. My husband was a

little spooked by this because we hadn't
learned anything yet about how our

loved ones Spirits' can be around.

So this began my introduction into the
Spirit world. Through the years, me and

my siblings all experienced different
little occurrences which we would share

and talk about. We would smell cigar
smoke suddenly just out of
nowhere...hear

knocking at the door and no one would be
there. We also would get hang up

phone calls and the TV would just shut
off suddenly and come back on just as

suddenly. That's when I started reading
all the books I could find about life

after death and those books pretty much
convinced me that this after life thing

is very real because these things were
happening to me and that our loved ones

can and do communicate with us and are
always around guiding us. This can

happen to anyone that lost a loved one,
you just need to learn the different

ways they use.

I am so glad that I have had these
experiences with my loved ones enough to

share them.

The next person to pass over was my mother. She was 70 years

old and had Ovarian Cancer. She died in the hospital. My siblings

and I kept a bedside vigil because the Doctor said it wouldn't be

long. I had taken a few days off from work so I could be at the

hospital more. All of us were there constantly, afraid that she

would pass without any of us being there. Although she was in a

Coma, she seemed to be holding her own and I decided to go back

to work and the rest of the family resumed their routines and we

decided to all take turns going to the hospital to be with her.

I worked at a Delicatessen and one day after returning to work, a

co-worker and I were cleaning up after the lunch rush when my

co-worker found an Earring. Turns out it was mine and somehow

just fell out of my ear. I was glad she found it because my

mother had given me those earrings.
This of course raised the

subject of how my mother was doing. I
decided to call the hospital

and speak to her Charge Nurse to see.
I was told to hold on and I'm

waiting and waiting and then her Doctor
got on the line and he said,

"I'm sorry to have to tell you this, but
your mother passed away a few

minutes ago". I know now that the
Earring was a sign I just didn't

know it then...I wonder now if the
Earring fell out at the time of her

death...it wouldn't surprise me.

One day I came home from work and in the
mail was a notice from my bank

saying that I had insufficient funds and
the account was one hundred and

forty four dollars short. I was so
worried because I didn't have the money

and pay day was still a few days away.

Awhile later, the phone rang, my
youngest son called me to the phone
saying

there was a man looking for my mother.
I grabbed the phone and this man said

he was from the hospital and was looking
for Patricia Henderson who was the

Beneficiary of Winifred Kiwin...that's
how he got my phone number. I was her

Beneficiary from when she lived with us
when she had gotten sick and my

siblings had all been in agreeance to it.
The man said he wanted to confirm

this information so he could send me a
check that her Insurance Company had

overpaid to the hospital. The amount of
the check was one hundred forty four

dollars!!! Wow! I was jumping for joy,
not only because this bailed me out

but, my mother came through and made
this happen...and this a year after her
death!

I started playing the number one forty
four and won on it a few times...thanks

Mom.

Later on that year, an aunt that my
mother had lived with before she had

gotten sick, asked my brother Jimmy to
come to her home because she was

selling it and found a few things
that belonged to my mother that she thought

we would want. So, Jimmy made the trip
down to South Jersey and stopped at

my house on his way back so I could look
through the stuff and choose what

I wanted. I took some pictures and a
few of her Purses. A few days later,

I decided to go through the purses. In
one of them I found a wallet. I looked

through it and in it were the usual ID
cards, but what caught my eye was a

lottery ticket...an old one but the
number really made my hair stand up..it

was 144!!!! Apparently my mother played
this number at one time. When she

lived with us in Little Falls before she
died, our house number was 144 but I

never knew she had played it, and we no
longer lived in that house...we

bought a house the year my mother died.
She never got to see it. That number

has a very special meaning to me now.

My daughter who was a teenager when my
mother died had this happen...Before

my mother died, my daughter had lost two
rings that my mother had bought her.

She used to wear these rings all the
time and together on the same finger.

They were both Gold, one was a heart and
one was a rose. My mother shared my

daughter's bedroom in the Little Falls
house because it was a large room and

she kept the rings on her dresser. One
day these rings just literally

vanished. My daughter looked everywhere
but they were nowhere to be found.

After my mother passed on, my daughter
and I were cleaning out my mothers

closet. My daughter pulled out a tote
bag that was my mother's and heard

this jingle sound. She looked inside
the bag but there was nothing in it.

She shook the bag and heard this
jingling sound again...opened the bag,
saw a

zipper, unzipped it and there were her
two rings! We knew immediately that

this was my mother! Again, we all
experienced little signs from our
parents

and we would all exchange our occurrences through
the years, but the next

passing would really rock us to the very
core of our souls.

I was sitting watching the eleven
o'clock news and heard my phone

ring. My son Scott was downstairs in
our basement watching TV and

answered it. He came flying upstairs
into my bedroom where I was

and very excitedly said, "Ma, there's a
guy on the phone that says

he's Uncle Danny and that Aunt Margie
died"! Oh my God! My heart

stopped and I hurried up and picked up
the phone. It was "Big Danny"

Margies' ex father-in-law confirming
this awful shocking news! I

could barely contain myself…Margie
just forty five years old! It

can't be true, but it was…worse in
fact. He told me that her children

had gone over to her apartment earlier
that night because they hadn't

heard from her in a few days and
couldn't reach her by phone. They

assumed she was at the beach because she
lived close to it and loved

living in Florida for that reason. When
they couldn't get a hold of

her for a few days, they started to
worry. That's when they decided

to take the twenty minute drive to her
apartment to see what was going

on. They knocked and knocked on her
door but no answer. They knew she

wouldn't be at the beach now because it
was dark out. They banged again

but nothing...they decided to go around
back and they found a window. They

broke in through the window and that's
when they saw her...in her bed obviously

not alive.

The last person who saw Margie alive was
a neighbor named Eric. He said they

spent Monday night sitting outside the
Apartment Complex having a few beers

and a few laughs. He said everything
seemed to be ok with her, she was happy

and looking forward to the arrival of
her boyfriend who was coming down in a

few days. He said they called it a
night around eleven o'clock or so and
both

went into their apartments. He said
that around one thirty or two o'clock

in the morning, Margie called him on the
phone and asked him to please come

over because she didn't feel too good
and had called an Ambulance, and in the

event she had to go to the hospital, she
wanted him to call her family to let

them know. He said that Margie
complained to the Ambulance attendants
of

having chest pain. The two dismissed
this as being Gas and told her to take

Riopan. The neighbor Eric went to a
Convienience Store and bought it for
her.

She thanked him, said she'd be ok, took
the Riopan and Eric left to go back to

his apartment.

He had no idea that Margie had died and
didn't think it was strange not seeing

her around all week because he assumed
she was busy getting ready for her

boyfriend's visit. He was shocked when
her kids told him that they had found

her and that's when he told them about
Monday night. This was now Thursday

March 3rd.

What was weird to me was, I had given my
husband a surprise Fiftieth Birthday

party at our home on Saturday February
26th. Margie knew all about it of

course and the plans I had which was me
and my husband taking our son Scott

out for dinner for Scott's birthday
which was coming up on Monday February

28th. All our other kids were home
greeting all the guests that were
invited

to the surprise party. Margie said she
would call around nine o'clock that

night giving us a chance to get back
from dinner and the surprise would
already

have happened and she'd then be able to
wish my husband a happy birthday and

say hello to the family, but she never
called. I thought that was very odd

because my husband was her favorite
brother-in-law and if she said she'd
call

she'd call...that was how Margie was. I
figured something must have come up.

The next day, Sunday I was busy cleaning
up from the party and getting ready to

cook a special meal for Scott for his
real birthday dinner when my niece Edie

called. She asked if Margie had called
yet and I said she hadn't. Edie

decided to call Margie...she called me
back and said she couldn't reach her.

She called Margie's daughter and
explained that she was trying to reach
her

mother but no answer. Her daughter
assured Edie not to worry, that Margie

probably went to the beach.

Monday I went to work and thinking no
news is good news I wasn't too concerned

about not hearing from Margie. She
would be working today too and usually
she

made all her phone calls on the weekend,
and I would know then why she
didn't
call.

Then that dreaded phone call on Thursday
night from Big Danny...I was just

floored! By law, the Coroners Office
had to do an Autopsy. The Autopsy said

she died from a massive heart attack and
they put the date of her death as

March 1, 1994 approximately two thirty
AM. Some gas pains! I was livid!

That meant that she lay dead from

Tuesday March first until Thursday

March third! Three days!!! Oh my God
poor Margie...all alone...unbelievable!

I knew that Margie would not want to be
buried in Florida as much as she loved

it. She had no Life Insurance and her
kids had no money to bury her either,

so my husband and I and my siblings all
chipped in and paid for her Funeral.

We also had to pay to fly her body up
here to New Jersey. Margie hated
flying,

she either drove with someone to Florida
or took a Grey Hound Bus, and now

in death she had no choice but to fly
and that REALLY bothered me. She was

Cremated, that was something her kids
said she definitely was clear about.

Her sudden death really rocked our
world. She was the baby of our family

and the first sibling to go. So young,
so much to live for, how could this

happen...only forty five years old. It
really rocked us siblings to our core.

I kept her Ashes till things calmed down
and sent some to her children in

Florida. The rest were put in the
ground at the Cemetery where our parents

and Margie's infant son Christopher's
lay in their final resting place. I
know

Margie would have approved.

I have had so many visits" from Margie
and I love that she comes around.

The first was a few months after her
death. I was cleaning out my bedroom

closet the end of February while she was
still alive. I was cleaning the house

and getting it ready for the Fiftieth
Surprise party for my husband. I
emptied

the entire closet out and had piles of
stuff that was garbage and piles of

stuff that I would be keeping. I put
all the stuff I was getting rid of in

a garbage bag and started to put
everything back in the closet. When the

clothes were put back, I started on the
shoes. I started putting shoes that

were out of their boxes back into the
boxes and back into the closet. I found

this one shoe and put it in its box but

I couldn't find the other one. I

figured it would turn up before I was
finished so I put that box aside. Upon

finishing I was putting the rest of the
stuff back when I realized I hadn't

found that other shoe. My first thought
was I must have thrown it in the bag

that I was getting rid of. I started
looking fast through the stuff I was

getting rid of, but nothing. By now I
was getting frustrated and was tired

and just wanted this chore to be done.
I went into my daughters' room...she

was off from work that day, I explained
my frustration about not being able

to find this one shoe and she could see
that I was getting very aggravated.

She came into my room, looked through
everything and dumped out the bag that I

was getting rid of, but nothing. It
couldn't

have gotten under my bed because I had a
water

bed that was on a platform. In any
case, I said

that I'm not throwing the one I have out
because

I had never worn them and they were new
and I

was sure the missing one would turn up somewhere.

I put the box with the one black shoe in
it back

into the closet and forgot about it.

A few months later, I was looking for
something

in my closet when something on the shelf
caught my

eye...a shoe...that black shoe that I
could swear I

put in its box and back in the
closet. I'm

thinking this as I grab it and get the
box it belonged in.

I get the box, open it and I gasped!
There was the shoe! I

DID put it back that day...so what was
this????

I screamed, "Oh my God"! My daughter
came running into my room

and I showed her the box with the shoe
and the one in my hand

that was on the shelf and she
immediately said, "Aunt Margie"!

What is so ironic about this is, me and
Margie used to Jitterbug

together all the time since we were seven and
nine years old and Margie always lead.

The shoe that she brought back was the
left one which is the foot you

start off with when you lead! I was so happy
that she came to me this way.

She knew that by using the shoe I would
definitely know it was her because

of us always dancing. I didn't know
then all the ways they use but I

found out since that they use things
that will make you know instantly

which loved one it is coming around.
That is how it gets validated.

There was no question about it, it was
Margie that took that shoe and

then returned it.

Thinking back to when I cleaned that
closet out, it being the end of

February just a few days before she
died, I now wonder if that missing

shoe was an omen of her impending death.

Sometime in the Fall of nineteen ninety
four, I had this dream that

my phone rang and I answered it and
although there was a lot of

static, it was Margie! I was so excited
to hear her voice.

I asked her if she saw Daddy yet and she
said, "No they won't

let me see him because he never returned
Freddie Dittamo's

records of the Ex-Fifth that he
borrowed". (Freddie Dittamo was

in the Drum Corp with my father). With
that, I hear this deep

loud booming voice announcing, "All
those that died from heart attacks line
up

here, all those that died from cancer,
line up here". Margie said, "I

have to go, but meet me Saturday, I'll
be on Kearney Street". She did say a

house number but I can't recall it.
Kearney Street is in Paterson, the city

we grew up in and in a neighborhood
that we lived in at one time.

Next thing I know, I'm walking with my
son Scott who is only about

four years old in this dream. I am very
excited because I am going to

see Margie who I know has passed on, but
hey, she called and told me she'd

be here, so I'm going. Me and Scott are
walking up and down Kearney Street

and I'm getting very frustrated because
I cannot find this house. Feeling

sad about that, I reluctantly decide to
give up looking when all of a sudden

we happen upon this house that I somehow
just know is the house where she

said she'd be. The house had a long
driveway on the left side of it and

we walked up it and the yard opened up
to the right and had a big tree in

the far corner and under this tree was Margie!
She was dancing and looked so

happy and healthy and young. I started
running toward her crying, "Margie

is it really you"? I grabbed her and
started hugging her and holding onto her

for dear life! She said, "Yes, it's
really me". She brought me inside this

house and she introduced me to this man
that was tall with blonde hair and

was wearing a Tweed top coat...very
nicely dressed and nice looking and she

said he was her boyfriend. She started
showing me through this house which

was empty. She said they had just
bought it. Then, next thing I know, we

are outside in the yard again and Margie
was inside this shed and all these

people were lined up from the driveway
to this shed to see her and were

going in one by one, to pay their
respects to her, much like in the movie,

"The Godfather". I remember feeling
disappointed because somehow I knew she

couldn't stay long and these people who I didn't know
were taking up all the

time I could be spending with her. Then
I heard this whirring sound and Margie

came out of the shed and said she had to
go...and this blue helicopter dropped

right into the yard and took her and the
blonde guy and up they went all this

time this whirring sound as they rose up.

Now I wake up from this dream and I
still hear this whirring sound and
although

I'm running the dream through my head, I
am well aware that this whirring sound

is right outside. I always have my
window slightly open even in the winter,
so

I heard this very clearly. I get up and
I notice it is four am. I peek out my

bedroom window and I see this big black
Cadillac parked across my driveway

just idling. My first thought was it's
the person delivering the newspaper,

so I stand there watching, waiting to
see this person either get out or get

in the car. A few seconds went by and
no one got in or out of that car and

with that, it slowly pulled away! I got
back in bed and tried to go back to

sleep but it bothered me that I didn't
see anyone get in or get out of that

car, yet, it pulled away.

The next morning, I kept thinking about
that dream. It was so real and it

really bothered me because for the time
I dreamed it, Margie was here, but

now that I'm awake and realize it was a
dream, it was a big let down.

I told my husband about this dream and
how it bothered me. A few weeks later,

I was still talking about this dream and
I wondered out loud if there was

anything to it because of Kearney Street
being a real tangible street that

wasn't far from where we lived now. My
husband said, "Ok...so you want to take

a ride over there to see what"? I said
I didn't know, but I just knew and felt

that I had to. So, off we go. We turn
left onto Kearney Street from Union

Ave. We proceed down Kearney
Street...nothing. We cross Crosby Ave
and

truthfully, I didn't know that this side
of Kearney Street existed. It's a

short stretch of it and dead-ends. We
ride down a few feet and all of a sudden

I see this house! I yelled,
"Stop...that's it"! By now we were past
it so

my husband rode to the dead-end and
turned around and we drove back up the

street and there it was...this was the
house! There was the driveway and the

yard was to the right of the driveway
and as we approached the corner of the

street, you could clearly see the big
tree in the far corner of the yard...the

tree that Margie was dancing under!!!
I could not believe it! Just as I had

dreamed. This house meant nothing to me
or to anyone else in the family and I

have never been able to connect this
house to Margie only in my dream....but

I really believe in my heart that the
connection I can make and wholeheartedly

believe is that the car I heard and saw
outside when I awoke from that dream,

was Margie coming to return that black
shoe she took! For now I know it and

I will still not give up looking to find
out what that house on Kearney

Street means. One day I hope to find
out.

My brother Willie was the next to pass
on. This just two years

after we lost Margie. He had been in
and out of the hospital

for awhile before that. The day before
he died, we were all

in the Emergency Room at the hospital
with him. He had been

having a lot of discomfort. They let us
all in and let us stay

because they knew he wouldn't be living
much longer. The next

morning he passed quietly. My brother
Jimmy was there, the rest

of us were enroute to the hospital.

We wanted music at his Wake, so my
brother Joe made a cassette tape...Band

Music including one favorite march that
Willie loved called "Regimental

Pride" and a beautiful rendition of
"Danny Boy" both by the West Point Band.

Joe made a full tape but put those two
songs back to back so they could

play one after the other for the Wake.
Both were played at the Wake when it

was time for everyone to go up and say
our final farewell. It was very sad,

but also beautiful and I know Willie
loved hearing those pieces. Someone

seated in the Funeral Parlor had a Penny
Whistle and quietly played "Danny

Boy". It was very touching.
Willie grew up around Drum Corp. My father

belonged to the Ex-Fifth Regiment Field Music
and both Joe and Willie loved the music

so both took music lessons. Joe became
a drummer and Willie played bugle and later

snare drum.
Joe said he filled both sides of the tape so I

could make copies for anyone that wanted one.
Willie's daughter Edie and his son, Billy both

wanted copies, so I had the job of making two tapes.
The day I decided to make these copies, I set up

my double cassette player/recorder downstairs in my
basement and left the door open so I could

hear the music while making the tapes. When both
tapes were finished on side one, I went downstairs

to flip both of the tapes over to play and record side
two. This player/recorder had to be done manually,

it didn't automatically switch to the second side. After
about a half an hour, the music stopped

indicating side two was now complete and the player stopped automatically so there was no hurry

for me to go downstairs right then. I figured I would finish what I was doing upstairs and then go down

and make the second copy. All of a sudden "Regimental Pride" starts playing! By itself! This

was so strange because that was the first March on side one of the tape and now both tapes were on

side two! My brother Joe put that March first and "Danny Boy" second, so they could be played one right after the other at the Wake. I just smiled and said, "Ok Willie, don't be scaring me right now..I

know you're here...love you".
Another very prevalent sign came from Willie about

six months after he passed. My sister Maureen and I would go frequently to the Cemetery to visit

all the Graves of our family. This one day, Willie's daughter Edie came with us. She wanted to see all

the old Graves of the family which would be her Great Grandparents. Willie had shown me a few

times where they were, but every time I tried to find them, I never could. I knew the general area they

were in, but I just could not find the exact location. I explained this to Edie as we were driving toward

that area and searching the names on the headstones.
After a few minutes of looking, I turned up this one
little street and was crawling very slowly so they could
scan the names on the

headstones looking for our family name when all of a
sudden out of nowhere this flock of birds just

landed in front of the car actually blocking my path!
as we're witnessing this, stunned by how

many birds there were, my sister Maureen
says, "Look, there's Grandma and

Grandpa's Grave". We look, and you
could clearly see our last name on the

Headstone. We all looked at each other
knowing it was Willie that lead us

there and now I find it very easily when
I go to the Cemetery.

My brother Joe passed on March 15, 1999.
I was deeply saddened when

his daughter Peggy called and told me.
Joe was a Drummer as long

as I can remember. He was a member of
the Ex-Fifth Regiment Field

Music as a young boy along with my Dad
and my brother Willie. Right

before he married his sweetheart Marge,
in the fifties, he auditioned

for the United States Military Academy
Band at West Point, New York,

and he and his new bride started their
life in Upstate New York, first

in Fort Montgomery and eventually moving
into quarters on Post at

West Point where by now he and Marge had
two daughters and a child

on the way, a son who was born at West
Point. Every four years Joe

would re-enlist in the Army and enjoyed
a twenty seven year career

with the Band and also in the
"Hellcats", the Field Music detachment

of the band. Joe loved West Point and
so did all of us. When I was

a young girl, my parents would go up
most Saturdays to see a Dress

Parade. We were so proud of Joe.

When Joe retired from the band in the
eighties, he retired at the rank

of Sergeant Major and he and Marge
bought a home in Highland Falls, right

outside of West Point. Joe still worked
part time at West Point in the

Commissary and Marge worked at the Point
also. Joe also kept active in

the music and was a member of a Fife and
Drum Corp from Newburgh, New York.

When Joe passed away, he was entitled to
be buried at the Cemetery on Post

at West Point. He also was entitled to
two Field Musicians to play at his

Funeral. When the notice of his Funeral
was posted at the Band Barracks,

quite a few of his "old comrades"
volunteered to play at his funeral.

It was a true Military Funeral...very
sad. We were escorted to chairs

that were set up at the cemetery. Once
everyone was seated and in place,

the Honor Guards opened the doors to the
Hearse and as soon as the Casket

was lowered into their hands, the band
started playing, "Army Blue"...very

slow and haunting. I thought my heart
would burst out of my chest. Everyone

was sobbing so loud and my brother James practically
fell against me so

wracked with grief. With that, the band
played, "America The Beautiful"

and then the Priest started the
blessing. A few minutes into the
service,

this bird perched itself right opposite
the Casket and stated squawking

so loud that you couldn't help but
notice it. This went on for practically

the entire service. Then the band played,
"Auld Lang Syne" and finally,

"Taps". He also had a gun salute. It
was very heartwrenching but so beautiful

a funeral fit for a King! This bird sat
up across from the Casket and just

kept squawking and then finally it flew
away. I believe it was Joe. I think

he wanted to let us know that he highly
approved of his funeral. He LOVED

West Point and everything it stood for.

He is buried right across from General
George Armstrong Custer. Joe loved

Custer and would be so pleased to be buried right
across from him.

After the funeral service, a Repast was
held on post at the Associate Of

Graduates building where Marge worked
for many years.

There were hundreds that attended the
funeral. The family agreed that the

squawking bird was definitely Joe and I
felt very happy about that because

it was comforting to know that even
though he had passed on, he was there

and knew exactly what was going on.

Of all the losses I've had, James's was
by far the worst. James was

only fifty eight years old. So much to
live for, but double

Pneumonia claimed his life.

He married the love of his life, Gloria
and they had four children

and four grandchildren, so his passing
being very sudden was a

tremendous shock and very heartbreaking.
He died in the hospital

he had been brought to by Ambulance
eight days earlier. None of

us had a chance to say goodbye because
his Doctor's put him into a

Drug induced Coma. This was supposedly
to help him breathe easier,

but all their sophisticated drugs
couldn't touch the bacterial infection

that claimed his life. I will never
forget the shock and utter disbelief

at hearing his daughter Debbie crying
hysterically on the phone that morning

at around four am telling me that her
father had died. How could this happen

in this day and age? How would we all
get through this? So devastating...as

if my heart was cut out of my chest!
This just eleven months after we buried

Joe!

He had a beautiful Wake and Funeral.
There were so many that came and paid

their respects.

His funeral was February 28th. I know
this because that was my son Scott's

birthday. I remember that morning at
the Funeral Home...we were all just

devastated and I wondered how we would
be able to contain ourselves from

the shock of it all.

When my son Scott arrived with his
girlfriend, he came over to me and told

me that on their way to the Funeral
Home, he was stopped at a traffic light.

While waiting for the light to change, a
balloon hit the windshield of his car.

It hit hard and he and his girlfriend
looked up at it...the balloon said,
Happy

Birthday"! I knew immediately that this
was from James. James was Scott's

Godfather. I felt good at hearing this
and by now, with all the losses I'd

had, I knew they come around and they
have ways to let you know it's them...

how much clearer a sign could that have
been! I immediately related this story

to James's widow Gloria and although it
brought tears flowing, she felt very
comforted hearing this. Everyone did.

James's Funeral Mass was beautiful and
as we were leaving Church, a Bagpiper

could be heard playing, "Minstrel Boy"
in the distance...sad but beautiful

and a favorite Irish tune of James's.

Since his passing, I've had many "visits" from him.
Before he passed
over, he

took a job driving a truck for NAPA Auto
Parts. I had never heard of them but

since James's passing, their trucks and
logo started showing up everywhere!

This happened to Gloria as well.

James's daughter Debbie had this happen:
She was driving on the highway and

was daydreaming...her mind just started
to drift and she was thinking about her

father. This car came upon her rather
quickly which got her attention and

snapped her out of her daydream. With
that, the car passed her...she was

shocked when she read the license plate.
It read J.K. and a few numbers.

J.K. are James's first and last name
initials! Debbie felt so good at having

this little visit from her father...she
couldn't wait to tell me.

All of sudden, I'd see commercials too
on TV for NAPA Auto Parts never saw

them before and trucks with the Napa
logo would turn up on the roads I'd be
on

all the time. I believe it was James
saying hi.

In two thousand four, I had to have an
MRI. I was petrified and I prayed to

James to please be with me for it. My
husband drove to the Medical Facility

in another town that we weren't too
familiar with, but we found it. We
pulled

into the parking lot. We parked the car
facing the street we had just turned

off of and right directly across the
street is this huge building that caught

my eye. The sign said NAPA Auto Parts!
I smiled and said to my husband, "Look

James is here...I know I'm in good hands
now". This meant the world to me and

just reinforced my belief that they can
and do come to visit us and are always

around us. We just have to be open to
it.
James was always a musician as well
as my Dad and my brothers, Joe and Willie.

I always loved the music of the Fife and
Drum and dreamed of becoming a

drummer. In May of nineteen ninety
four, that dream came true...thanks to

James. He had recently retired from his
job and I asked him if he would teach

me how to drum. He said he would and
within a year, James and I started a

Fife and Drum Corp. We picked up my
husband and a nephew that James also

taught and we had my brother Willie who
had become a Drummer years earlier.

A drum line only, but it was a start of
a life long dream of mine. James named

us The Sons And Daughters Of The Ex5th Regiment
because we were all offspring

of my Dad who was in the original Ex-
Fifth from the nineteen thirties until

nineteen sixty. Later on, I learned how
to play the Fife and we had a few

nieces that learned as well and we
became a full fledged Corp. We enjoyed

our time playing Parades and going to
Ancient Fife and Drum Musters.

In May of two thousand, our Corp played
in the Memorial Day Parade in spite

of our deep grief and being without our
"leader" and signature drummer, James.

There was someone walking along the
parade route with us and taping us, so
we

could have the Corp on tape. As we
turned off the main street onto this
side

street, we were playing "Over There".
The parade comes to a stop a little ways

down this street to have a short
ceremony and place a wreath on a War

Monument and to play "Taps". We were
marking time while still playing and

almost finished when you could hear this
horn blowing. It was pretty intense

it lasted a few seconds. This was so
ironic to me because the street that it

was coming from was just to our right
where we were marking time and this

street is the street where my sister
Margie and my mother had lived on many

years before. I realized later when I
heard the tape that not only were we

stopped at the street where Margie and
my mother had lived, but we were playing

"Over There" which was the signature
song of the original Ex-Fifth of which

my Dad, Willie and Joe were all members
of years prior! I knew it was all of

them...my Mom, Dad, Margie, Willie, Joe
and James letting us know they were

there. Also these cars could not move
into the street in between divisions

of the parade because there was no cross
street, only a left or a right turn

and they would be driving right into the
marchers, so they had to stay put.

So what was the horn blowing about?

I remember going to that same parade as
a kid in that same town to see Dad,

Willie and Joe with the Ex-Fifth and see
them coming down the street playing,

"Over There"...unbelievable!

Us playing "Over There" at the same time
the car was blowing its horn was pure

coincidence, it wasn't planned. So I

know that was just one more testament to

their coming to say hi.

James always said, "Keep the faith". I
never heard anyone else say that. A

few years ago on my birthday, I was
really feeling down. I asked James to
come

around for my birthday to say hi. A few
hours later, I was on my computer and

went to this game I always play. It's a
board game with nine players...your

Screen name is listed just below the
game. The game won't start until there

are nine players or a minute goes by.
The last player's screen name was

KeepTheFaith! I just smiled and said.
"Thanks James". I yelled for my

husband to come quick...he came running
in and I told him to look at the last

persons' screen name. He too smiled and
said, "James".

My sister Maureen joined the others in October, 2005.

I haven't had too many "visits" from her, but I know she comes around. I could be sitting in my parlor doing nothing and all of a sudden I will smell her perfume. Other times I will hear a certain song that will remind me of her. I've also found a lot of my pictures being crooked and I have to straighten them. I know that's Maureen saying hi because she was a fanatic about pictures being straight. You cannot make your loved ones come, but they will let you know when they do. My daughters' TV would turn on and off all the time when Maureen first passed. Then it stopped. It happened again on the first anniversary of her passing. My daughter was close to Maureen and prays to her all the time.

In July, 2008, Maureen's oldest son, Billy and his new wife, Paula came out to New Jersey to visit family and friends.

We spent the day together and talked and laughed and shared a lot of "Maureen" stories. Maureen had left NJ and moved in with Billy in 2000 and lived with Billy in California until her death. We laughed the whole time they were here. Their visit was a short one due to many friends and other relatives they planned on visiting, but I was happy to see Billy and to meet Paula. The next day, I got up, did my usual...go online with my coffee for a little while and then signed off to start my housework.

As I started to make my bed, I noticed that my 37 inch flat screen TV was now catty-corner instead of just being straight on the console table it sits on. I yelled out to Bill who was in the parlor asking if he turned it.

He said, "No". I really knew in my heart that he wouldn't have turned it...what would be the point of turning it away from being able to see it from the bed. Then it hit me...Maureen!!! She had a habit in life of catty-cornering everything. She could change the look of a room just by catty-cornering something...

I do it too…she always taught me that. She was letting me know that she was around and that she knew her son had been here with his new wife.

I was so happy she came around.

Aside from my daughter being close to Maureen, she was also very close To Margie. The night we got the call that Margie passed, she went into her bedroom and as she walked in, the TV just came on! The remote was on her bed and as fast as it came on; it shut off! By now, with all the losses we've had, and all the "visits" I've had, my daughter was witness to a lot of them, so she wasn't surprised that Margie and Maureen came to her.

My husband had an occurrence when Margie passed.

We were planning her funeral and my husband woke up in the middle of the night with words in his head that he wrote down. We were shocked that he could even remember them because he never remembers any dreams. He always says he doesn't dream. The dream he had was sketchy but the words were unbelievable.

The words were a Poem that said:

Margie

Always the life of the party
Always the last one to leave
Now you're the first one in Heaven
Leaving us down here to grieve
Your children are all here to see you
Your brother's and sister's are too
Your nieces, nephews, cousins and friends
Are all here to bid you adieu
Someday we'll all come to your party
But until we all see you again
You'll be in our hearts forever
A good mother, good sister, good friend.

I was totally floored that my husband could not only dream these words, but remember them! I wanted this read at her Wake, I was so proud of him.

The Funeral Director told all how this poem came to my husband through a dream.

Everyone was so touched by the poem. One of my nieces had it done up in Calligraphy and found a picture of Margie and had it framed with a circle cut-out for Margie's picture with the poem right next to it. It now hangs on my wall where I look at it all the time. I also have all their pictures on my wall right by my computer, and I feel as though they are around me.

The bond that we shared with each other can never be severed by death. I carry them all in my heart.

The latest sign I had from my loved ones came just last week, February 15th, 2009. My friend Lana Director who wrote the poem encouraged me to get this book published. I asked my loved ones for a sign. I asked them to let me know if they knew I had written a book and if I should publish it. The number 24 kept coming into my head...at first nothing...then I knew.

My brother Jimmy passed February 24th, so I knew right away that they knew of the book....but the best was, I had received an E-mail from Dorrance Publishers on February 16th asking me to submit my manuscript! As I write this today, February 22, 2009 I am planning on mailing this out on the 24th, my brother Jimmy's ninth anniversary in Heaven and I know that the date and the email were a sign from him. When I first wrote this book, I had gotten a list of Publishing Companies, but I never pursued submitting so I am further convinced by the email that they want me to publish it.

Thanks Jim!